The Missed Mission

When the Church Forgets Its True Calling

Comfort Ekundayo

Editing, cover design and author services by Opulent Books: www.OpulentBooks.net

ISBN: 978-1-916691-27-8

Dedication

To my beloved husband,

I thank God every day for the precious time we shared. Our 45 years of marriage were profound and purpose-filled before you went to be with the Lord. You were more than just my husband; you were my pillar, always there, always supporting me.

I glorify God for the gift of you in my life. Your legacy of faith and love continues to inspire me.

Acknowledgements

First and foremost, I'd like to express my deepest gratitude to my daughter, Olayinka. Your encouragement was the spark that ignited the journey of writing this book.

A heartfelt thank you to Kensington Temple, my spiritual home for 14 formative years. The teachings, guidance, and fellowship I received there have shaped me in more ways than I can express.

To Pastors Wynne Lewis and Colin Dye, your leadership and wisdom have been light in my spiritual journey.

I'd like to acknowledge Rev. Morris Cerullo for his profound teachings and impact. His insights and dedication to spreading the word of God have left an indelible mark on my heart and soul.

I extend my heartfelt gratitude to Pastor Sunday Adelaja for his invaluable teaching. His guidance and wisdom have been instrumental in shaping my ministry.

I also want to thank Joe Benjamin, my book coach, and publisher, along with his team, for their dedication and support throughout this journey. Their expertise and commitment have been integral to the realisation of this work.

To everyone mentioned and to countless others who have touched my life, directly or indirectly, thank you. This book is a testament to the collective wisdom, love, and grace I've been fortunate to receive.

Lastly I give thanks to God, the giver of life, wisdom, understanding, and knowledge, for guiding me throughout the process of creating this life-changing book.

Table of Contents

Introduction

On a bright, bustling day, I found myself standing on a street corner, passionately sharing the gospel. The urban noise around me, the curious glances from passers-by, and the occasional nod of acknowledgment were all too familiar. But on this day, a particular encounter shook me to my core. A woman, with tears streaming down her face, confessed how she once did what I was doing but had drifted away from the church. Her story was not unique; it echoed the experiences of many souls I had met.

My heart brims with gratitude to God for His unending mercy upon my life and my family. Compelled by an inner urge, I have always been drawn to preach the gospel of the Lord Jesus Christ. This book, birthed from deep reflections and encounters, is a witness to my journey in the church and an urgent appeal for change.

I've witnessed pain and confusion within the church walls. Countless 'sheep' wander aimlessly, lost amidst rituals and numbers, yearning for genuine guidance and mentorship. A Muslim woman in my last church, for instance, felt like a fish out of water. The community seemed unprepared to guide her. It was these instances, these souls drifting away, that deeply pained me. At times, I felt like we were merely catching fish, only to toss them back into the vast ocean, unattended and unguided.

The root of my message? The church, in its zeal

for evangelism, often forgets the critical second step: nurturing and caring for the souls it brings in. We pray fervently for new souls to join us, but are we prepared to support them in their spiritual journey? We must cleanse our sanctuaries of anything that drives people away from Christ. Without a strategic plan for nurturing, our efforts are in vain. Has the church missed its mission?

John 14:12 says, "*He that believeth in me, the works that I do shall he do also; and greater works than these shall he do.*" As believers, we must employ Jesus' teachings, understanding His intention to multiply, not merely increase numbers. True growth is measured by spiritual depth, not by headcount. We must inspire individuals to grow beyond us, not be content with mere membership.

In this book, I share my experiences, my observations, and most importantly, my call for a shift in focus. From mere evangelism to genuine discipleship. From counting numbers to nurturing souls. From holding on tightly to setting people free to fulfil God's purpose in the world.

Chapter 1

Early Church Life

In the heart of the ancient city of Jerusalem, amidst fervent prayers, the early church thrived in a realm of unprecedented power. Their gatherings filled with faith and anticipation, rooted in the promise foretold by the scriptures. Acts 2:1-12 was not merely a recounting of events but a testimony of the profound transformation that awaited those who dared to believe.

In the quiet moments before the rushing wind and the tongues of fire descended upon them, the disciples were beckoned by the words of Jesus Himself. Acts 1:8 says "*But ye shall receive power, after that the Holy Ghost is come upon you: and ye shall be witnesses unto me both in Jerusalem, and in all Judaea, and in Samaria, and unto the uttermost part of the earth.*"

They had a command to tarry, to congregate in the holy city, and to wait expectantly for the fulfilment of a Divine promise. They didn't comprehend the exact form this promise would take – whether it be tongues of fire or the gift of tongues.

Their anticipation was not for the spectacular manifestations but for the revelation that Jesus, their Messiah, had indeed risen and was alive. It was a moment of unity, faith, and expectancy, as they gathered in unison, seeking the unveiling of God's plan.

The coming down of Power upon the early church through the Holy Spirit was indeed pivotal in enabling them to fulfil their mission. This Divine Empowerment was not merely for personal or internal spiritual growth but served as a catalyst for the outward propagation of the Gospel and making disciples.

The question then is, has the church missed its mission? I will get more into this in the coming chapters.

The idea that the church might have "missed" its mission doesn't necessarily imply complete failure but rather prompts introspection and a call for re-evaluation. It invites a critical examination of whether the church is still aligned with its initial purpose of proclaiming the Gospel, making disciples, fostering unity, and serving as a beacon of

Christ's love to the world.

This contemplation serves as a reminder for the church to continually reassess its priorities, realign its focus with the teachings of Christ, and strive for a more vibrant, impactful, and faithful representation of its mission in an ever-changing world.

Reflecting on my upbringing, I've witnessed a noticeable contrast between the church of my childhood and the present-day contemporary church. Allow me to share a glimpse of my formative experiences that shaped my perspective.

A Legacy Of Faith

My family's spiritual legacy traces back to the revival in Okeoye, Ilesha, Osun State, Nigeria, where my grandparents devoted their lives to God during the 1930s revival. This profound commitment to faith shaped my upbringing significantly. I spent much of my early life attending church alongside my grandparents, a tradition that persisted throughout my years.

Our routine revolved around the church, becoming a fundamental part of our daily lives. We attended services both in the mornings and evenings on weekdays, excluding only Saturdays and Sundays. Mornings commenced with an early 6 AM church service before heading to work, and back to church after work. This formed a pattern where we began our day immersed in the house of the Lord.

The prevalent influence of God's presence made attending church an effortless and uplifting experience; it never felt like a burden or obligation. Church was part of daily life and made us the people we are today. This was in line with the biblical exhortation found in Hebrews 10:25, which encourages believers to assemble and meet together as a unified church body. *"Not forsaking the assembling of ourselves together, as the manner of some is; but exhorting one another: and so much the more, as ye see the day approaching."*

The early Christians continued to meet daily, both in the temple and in their homes. They shared meals together, rejoiced in unity, praised God, and their gatherings were accompanied by the growth of the church through the addition of new believers. Acts 2:46-47 *"And they, continuing daily with one accord in the temple, and breaking bread from house to house, did eat their meat with gladness and singleness of heart, praising God, and having favour with all the people. And the Lord added to the church daily such as should be saved."*

In today's context, meeting daily as the early

church did in the book of Acts might seem impractical or challenging due to the pace of modern life.

Relocation to England

After several years, I made the decision to immigrate to the United Kingdom. However, upon my arrival, I noticed a significant difference in the church environment compared to what I had experienced before. Initially, I struggled to find a community similar of the vibrant church I had known. My search led me to various churches in London, hoping to rediscover that spiritual connection I once felt.

Eventually, I stumbled upon churches that appeared similar, yet as I became involved, I realised they weren't quite the same. These congregations predominantly gathered solely on Sundays, creating a noticeable gap from the continuous fellowship I had grown up with. It felt like there was something missing, a sense of deeper spiritual connection and commitment.

It became apparent that many of these churches seemed to lack the fervour for spiritual empowerment that I had witnessed before. Instead, the focus seemed to lean more towards using the congregation rather than empowering them. There was a stark absence of the earnest pursuit of God's presence and the embodiment of Christ's teachings.

In general, it seemed as though the contemporary church was not primarily seeking spiritual empowerment or embodying the heart of Jesus. Instead, there appeared to be a shift towards seeking what members could contribute or provide for the church's benefit, rather than nurturing a community rooted in the essence of Christ's teachings.

The book of John 14:12 states:

"Verily, verily, I say unto you, He that believeth on me, the works that I do shall he do also; and greater works than these shall he do; because I go unto my Father."

In this verse, Jesus speaks to His disciples, emphasising that those who believe in Him will perform the works that He did and, astonishingly, even greater works. Jesus promises that believers will accomplish remarkable deeds empowered by their faith, as He is going to the Father.

Jesus assured his disciples of an extraordinary promise, empowering them to perform the miraculous deeds He had done and even surpass them. He healed the sick, performed miracles, fed the hungry, and demonstrated God's power, including raising the dead. This assurance of greater works was bestowed upon his followers.

In contrast to this promise, today's church landscape often appears to prioritise serving the leaders rather than enabling individuals to fulfil their unique purposes in life. Many individuals within church congregations have seemingly lost sight of their individual callings and life purposes. Stagnation has crept into the lives of numerous church members, observed first-hand in the community I belonged to.

Tragically, I've witnessed individuals passing away without fully realising or fulfilling their God-given calling. It has become evident that many are stagnant within the confines of church structures, failing to grasp their personal destinies.

The time has come for members to awaken, seeking a personal encounter with God. Each individual must rise up and earnestly seek their purpose in communion with God. It's a crucial moment for personal introspection and reconnecting with God on an individual level.

My experiences within the church led me to a point where I ceased sharing my struggles with church leaders and respected figures in the faith. I had hoped for their support, yet instead, I encountered numerous internal battles. It grieves me to acknowledge that, in my view, many churches, consciously or inadvertently, collaborate with forces that hinder God's intended purpose on Earth. I continue to bring this concern before God.

Had it not been for the solid foundation laid in my early years, I might have been inclined to turn away from God due to the challenges I faced within the realm of spiritual leadership. My earnest prayer remains focused on the restoration of the church, a return to fervently seeking the power of God through prayer.

I firmly believe that unless the Church rekindles its pursuit of God's power and prioritises prayer, it will struggle to fulfil God's purpose on Earth. Regrettably, numerous churches gauge their success by the size of their congregations rather than the number of lives they've empowered to fulfil their God-given purposes.

I've been in situations where Pastors planned to avoid supporting another Pastor. It seems the church has become more like a business, with many Pastors competing and not uniting to lead the church. They're afraid to work together due to jealousy.

I've witnessed gatherings of Pastors where they pray negatively against other Pastors, and it's disheartening. I wonder, what kind of God are they truly serving? Unfortunately, many members in the church are unaware of what their Pastors are doing.

We need a renewal, a filling of God's power, to change this. It's essential for us all to come together and focus on the true purpose of serving God.

Chapter 2

The Conversion Of My Husband

I want to share with you about someone very special to me – my husband. His life story is a perfect example of how powerful the Gospel can be in changing lives. He embodies what the church's mission should be all about: helping people find their purpose as followers of Christ.

Seeing how he's transformed has shown me the incredible impact the Gospel can have. It's not just about changing a life – it's about igniting a sense of purpose and direction. Through his journey, I've witnessed first-hand how the Gospel can empower individuals to walk as devoted disciples of Christ.

His story is a living testimony to the life-changing power of the Gospel. It's a reminder that the Gospel isn't just a message; it's a force that reshapes and revives lives, guiding individuals towards a more meaningful and purposeful existence.

When I first met my husband, his family had Christian roots from a Methodist Church. His father and relatives were actively involved in the Methodist faith. However, after we married, he didn't actively engage in church practices, though he held spiritual beliefs that weren't deeply rooted in the Lord.

Upon joining him in London, I found that he wasn't attending any church at all. Coming from a Christian household where church life was integral from a young age, it was a significant part of my life. Nonetheless, I encouraged him to accompany me, and to my delight, he never declined. His willingness to attend church with me and our children brought me immense joy.

We eventually found a church where he joined me regularly. All our children were born in church and together, we endeavoured to raise them in the knowledge and reverence of the Lord.

Mission To London Encounter

Morris Cerullo would visit London annually for a Mission to London Crusade. In 1992, both my husband and I attended one of these events.

At that time, I knew my husband's prayers lasted no more than two or three minutes at most, and I earnestly prayed for him. I prayed, asking the Lord to let him experience a true encounter. Then, during the Morris Cerullo Mission to London that year, a remarkable event occurred. Sitting beside me, when the altar call was made, he rushed forward on the first day. I was amazed and thanked God.

On the second day, he responded again during the altar call, making a confession. I wasn't entirely sure what he said or did, but I knew it was a Divine intervention. Astonishingly, on the third day, he went forward once more. I was puzzled but asked him why he went forward again. He shared that he felt compelled to do so. It was then, on that third day, that he fully committed his life to Christ.

Following that Mission to London, everything changed. I witnessed a remarkable transformation in him. He began reading the Bible regularly, which was something entirely new. It was as if a new chapter had opened in his life. The teachings and experiences during the Mission to London had a profound impact, bringing about a profound change. He became a new person, embodying the truth of being in Christ and leaving behind his former self. From that point forward, he diligently read the Bible every day.

The Bible declares in 2 Corinthians 5:17, "*Therefore, if anyone is in Christ, the new creation has come: The old has gone, the new is here!*" Witnessing this transformation firsthand in my husband's life was proof to the extraordinary power of the Gospel. It's a power unlike any other, capable of turning lives upside down and ushering in a profound and lasting change. The truth of that scripture became vividly real to me as I saw my husband's life being completely renewed, illustrating the incredible impact and transformative force inherent in the Gospel of Christ.

My husband dedicated an hour every morning to God. Each day, as we rose, he'd head to a room, take his Bible, and immerse himself in its pages. He would quietly absorb its teachings, applying them to his own life and transformation. Despite his reserved nature, the change brought about by Christ in him was unmistakable. His words carried a new authority and power, often quoting scriptures that spoke directly to our hearts.

One particular day, he began to recite John 14:12 fervently. He urged me, saying, "Come and listen, darling, Jesus gave us power to do what He could do!" He marvelled at Jesus' words, highlighting that everyone could do what Jesus did. He believed that Jesus, opened the door for all to partake in such power. He repeated this sentiment for many weeks, and I thanked the Lord for this profound change in his life.

Being the sole one devoted to prayer in our family, witnessing this transformation brought immense joy to my life. His newfound zeal allowed him to embody the scriptures he held dear. The Word of God had ignited a fire within him, driving him to dig deeper. We attended Bible school together, and he embraced the training eagerly, igniting a significant change not just in his life but in our prayer life collectively.

Our yearly attendance at the Mission to London became a tradition. Each visit became a milestone, marking our continued growth and transformation in Christ.

Following his conversion, the work of God became an integral part of my life. For around 13 to

14 years, I led a cell group at Kensington Temple. Then, in 1995, when I joined Kensington Temple, I initiated another active cell group. In this new group, I guided the women while my husband led the men. His life remained deeply influenced by this until his final days.

It brought immense joy to witness this change in my husband's life. He had a remarkable ability to use scriptures that deeply resonated with him as a source of great inspiration and passion. The Word of God ignited a fervour within him that was truly palpable. We attended Bible school together and then pursued most of the subsequent training courses as a team. This collective experience changed our lives. As a result, not only did our prayer lives change, but our entire approach to prayer underwent a significant transformation.

We celebrated our 45th wedding anniversary in

2016, and tragically, my husband passed away on February 28, 2017. His departure was peaceful; he wasn't unwell, yet it seemed as if it was his appointed time to leave, having reached the vibrant age of 89. He remained incredibly active until just a few days before his passing.

His conversion had been a profoundly impactful and life-altering experience. Despite not being an outspoken individual, he found his unique way of spreading the gospel. He would gently share his faith with anyone he encountered, explaining, in his own manner, the importance of acknowledging Jesus as Lord. He quietly preached the gospel in his own way.

Throughout our time together, he actively supported me in various endeavours, particularly in evangelism. We jointly initiated a monthly Saturday meeting in Ilford, London for people to gather and engage in discussions. His solid support served as a strong backbone, always standing by my side, rarely seen, but incredibly supportive.

Chapter 3

Obedient Departures

In life, there are moments when a subtle whisper, a gentle nudge, or an inexplicable feeling prompts us to go somewhere or leave a familiar place. We've all experienced those peculiar sensations—the unmistakable tugs that seem to come from beyond our understanding.

In the Bible there is the story of Evangelist Philip, an ordinary man thrust into extraordinary circumstances, guided not by maps or plans but by a Higher Calling. He was called by the Holy Spirit to an encounter that would forever alter the course of another's life. The truth is our journeys are not mapped by our own designs but by Divine direction.

On a dusty road, a traveller an Ethiopian eunuch engrossed in ancient scrolls, met an evangelist on a mission. It's in this collision of destinies that we witness the beauty of obedience to the Spirit's leading.

Philip, like you and me, was not immune to uncertainty or hesitation. Yet, when the Holy Spirit nudged him to *'arise and go toward the south'* (Acts 8:26), he obeyed the voice of God, setting forth on a path that would lead to a Divine appointment.

In a world where GPS and detailed itineraries often dictate our travels, Philip used Divine navigation - guidance of the Holy Spirit. His story is an example to us to be obedient even in departure.

We're all travellers on this journey of faith, encountering crossroads where decisions to stay or depart present themselves. Stay humble and obedient to what the Holy Spirit tells you to do about the place you are called to serve and to worship Him.

Founding Member Of Church

My first experience was in a church in London, where I started attending even though it wasn't exactly the same as before in Nigeria. I felt the Lord guiding me there, so I went with my family and a few others who were part of the church's beginnings. We were a small group and made decisions together to help the church grow and bring more people in.

Initially, we gathered in a member's living room as the church began to grow. We had some leaders, including Bible students from Nigeria, who assisted us until they returned to Nigeria. Every year, students from a Bible school in England came to support and guide us in leading the church.

As foundational members, we shared the responsibility for everything in the church. Sometimes, we hosted visiting Pastors or leaders from Nigeria at our homes. Our time was largely dedicated to church activities, ensuring things ran smoothly.

As the church grew, we saw a steady influx of individuals, each bringing their own aspirations. What struck me profoundly in this growing community was the increasing focus on securing influential positions within the church. It became evident that many newcomers were driven by a desire for power and status.

Initially, when the church comprised mostly women with only a few men, a shift occurred. Some began to assert that women should not occupy positions on the committee. Consequently, the women who had played pivotal roles in establishing the church willingly stepped down to allow the men to take charge.

I stepped down. While I respected the leadership's decision, it didn't align with my belief rooted in the clear teachings of the Bible: in Christ, there is no male or female (Galatians 3:28).

Miracle in The Church

As the church continued to grow, we had evangelists from Nigeria's headquarters visit London to help us raise funds for our own building. It was incredible to witness the financial miracles that followed. Somehow, we managed to find someone in the bank willing to lend us money for purchasing our place of worship in London. It felt like a miracle, especially considering we only had £2000 in our accounts, yet we were aiming to buy a building worth £200,000 at the time.

I couldn't believe it was possible in human terms, but God showed me that He can do the impossible according to His Word. At that time, my husband served as the treasurer. It was truly a miracle of God's provision.

However, challenges emerged within the church. People were keen on positions and leadership roles, causing significant trouble. There were constant conflicts, almost every six months, leading to internal disputes and fights. The church was slowly missing its mission. I prayed earnestly, asking the Lord if this was what He had intended for the church. Eventually, after seeking Divine guidance, the Lord instructed me to leave the church.

Time For Departure

I felt it was time to leave. I prayed and asked the Lord where I should go. I didn't receive a clear answer immediately. Later, someone else gave a me a vison that I needed to move – which was confirmation. I left without knowing where I should be headed. Despite persuasion from others, I was certain that I had to depart. However, I made a mistake—I didn't pray to know where I should go. I simply went to another church. Initially, I was enthusiastic about this new church, but soon, the Holy Spirit prompted me that it wasn't where I was meant to settle. I realised I couldn't keep moving around. The lesson is; pray for guidance about where to go and God will show you.

After visiting two churches, I decided to stop wandering. I prayed earnestly, asking the Lord to show me where I should be. I asked a fellow believer to join me in prayer and fasting on a Saturday. During that time, the Lord directed me to go to Kensington Temple. Despite the distance, I obeyed. As I sat at the back of the church, I wondered how I could manage to come here regularly with my children. Then, something amazing happened.

The Pastor, after finishing the earlier service, unexpectedly returned to the pulpit during the next service at 11 o'clock. He mentioned that someone had been praying for guidance and had just arrived at the church. He declared that God had a plan for this person, urging them to stay, pray, and fulfil their calling within the church. It was an affirmation of what the Lord had revealed to us during our prayers on Saturday.

Bloom Where You Are Planted

If God plants you in a garden, flourish and bloom in that place. There is grace to thrive and grow, in any circumstances where you find yourself because God planted you there. Make the best of the situation and flourish spiritually, regardless of where you are in your journey or which church community you find yourself in.

Even if you're uncertain about whether you're in the exact place God wants you to be, you can still contribute positively, learn, and impact others while trusting in God's guidance.

A Bible verse that aligns with this is Colossians 3:23-24 "*And whatsoever ye do, do it heartily, as to the Lord, and not unto men; Knowing that of the Lord ye shall receive the reward of the inheritance: for ye serve the Lord Christ.”*

This verse encourages us to wholeheartedly dedicate ourselves to the tasks set before us, recognising that ultimately, we serve the Lord in all we do. Even if unsure about our specific placement, we can diligently serve God and others, trusting that He will guide us and bring about growth and fruitfulness in due time.

I stayed put, and that’s why I remained there for many years. I felt blessed by the church. I attended ministry training, revivals, and everyday activities to learn more. The power of God was moving so strongly during those times, teaching me to obey God. Often, we stick to one church because it feels comfortable. We might resist moving when God wants us to, and that can make us spiritually stuck.

Sometimes, especially when God has a specific plan for us, we can’t stay in one place. He might need us to move. I experienced this when God nudged me to leave my first church. It was eye-opening, exposing me to various church environments. Some things surprised me because I was deeply committed to serving God. I only wanted to serve Him with zeal. However, I learned that being in the right place at the right time matters. I hadn't realised this until I moved around and prayed for God's guidance.

When I prayed and God showed me where to go next, it was powerful. I was profoundly impacted by the teachings and was given opportunities to lead and use my gifts among people. Reflecting on it now, if I had stayed in the wrong place, I wouldn't have grown as much as I did. My life changed, and I deepened my understanding of the Word of God. I even had the privilege to teach leadership training and children. God opened many doors for me, teaching me the importance of understanding that our time in one place might have limits.

Obedience in Staying Put

Sometimes God will tell you to stay, but sometimes He will tell you to leave. When God instructs you to stay, it's crucial to heed that call and remain where you are, even in the face of challenges that might tempt you to leave.

I faced difficulties in my church that could have driven me away, but I stayed put because I believed it was what the Lord wanted. I waited until it was clearly another call to move on before I left. As Christians, obedience to God is vital in every aspect of our lives.

God doesn't intend for us to remain stagnant in one place for 20 or 30 years, as some may suggest. If God has a purpose for us, staying in one situation or position for a lifetime may hinder us from fulfilling that purpose. We must recognise that God is always moving and calling us forward. Failing to follow God's direction could cause us to miss His plans for us.

I am grateful for God's guidance in my life. At times, I didn't understand fully why God's purpose weighed so heavily on my heart, but I desired to please Him and move in the right direction. However, there were moments when I struggled and yearned to stay in one place, missing my friends and the familiar. Nonetheless, I had to follow where God was leading me and it brought peace.

Chapter 4

How God Used My Experience

My life within the church was a mixture of joy, sorrow, triumphs, and trials. I have encountered both challenging and rewarding experiences in the church, shaping my journey with its ups and downs. I firmly believe that God has a purpose for choosing me, and my life's experiences hold significance. It's why I'm writing this book—

to share my story and shed light on these issues, aiming to assist someone else on their journey. I strongly hold onto the truth that what I've been through, the highs and lows, will ultimately work together for good, as Romans 8:28 declares, "*And we know that all things work together for good to them that love God, to them who are the called according to his purpose.*"

Throughout my life, I've been both a visitor and a member of various churches. However, I never intended to journey from one church to another. As I reflect on my experiences, it became evident that God was orchestrating this path. Each transition brought forth new lessons; in every little place I found myself, there was something to learn. God continually captured my attention, guiding me in unexpected ways. Looking back, I'm grateful that He made these transitions to foster growth in my spiritual life.

God used my experiences to shape me into someone who spreads His word. In my earlier church, we didn't focus much on telling others about Jesus. We talked and invited people, but it wasn't a big thing there. Then, I moved to a different church, maybe the first or second one after that. This church was very passionate about going door to door to talk about Jesus. I felt delighted to join them. Every Saturday, we went out, even though it was a bit far, but I made my way there. We would knock on people's doors in groups and share about Jesus. They taught us how to do it. I enjoyed it a lot because I'd never done it in a group before; usually, it was one-on-one. We ministered to many people, and I saw some of them accept Jesus. I felt so thankful to the Lord; if I'd stayed in another church, I might not have had this chance to be with other believers doing this kind of work. Sadly, some bad things happened in the evangelism team, so we had to stop for a while. But during that short time, I learned a lot and got great experience talking to people about Jesus Christ.

Gifts Set To Use

In my journey through different churches, there was one where the Pastor stood out for his openness to the Holy Spirit. This church was unlike any other I had seen before. The Pastor was remarkably humble, leaving no room for pride. It was a place where my gifts were nurtured. My husband and I attended Bible college there, learning how to minister and preach. We spent several years in that church, and I learned a vital lesson about following God's call.

The Pastor was the kind who acted on God's

instructions without hesitation. If he felt God wanted something spoken, he'd say, "Just go up there and deliver the message." One day, I felt a Divine prompting unlike any other. It was as if God was urging me to warn the people in the church. The Pastor seemed to sense this too, handing me the microphone and saying, "Here's your moment Comfort, speak to the people as God leads you."

As I stepped forward, it was as if the heavens had opened above me. The words I spoke weren't mine; they flowed with a power beyond me. There was an overwhelming conviction in the air. People responded, coming forward to repent and give their lives to God. It was an experience unlike any other, a moment when I surrendered entirely to God's will. In that church, the Pastor was obedient to God's voice, which allowed me to operate in the gift God had given me.

It was a transformative moment—one where I realised that any fear of messing up wasn't mine to carry. This Pastor, by obeying God's voice, created an atmosphere where God's power could work wonders. The place buzzed with emotion; tears flowed freely; hearts were moved. That moment marked a significant turning point in my journey, showing me the incredible impact of obeying God's call without hesitation.

Leadership Sensitivity To The Holy Spirit

Leaders that are open to the Holy Spirit will make a difference in the church. There are several examples in the Bible of leaders who were sensitive to the Holy Spirit. One such example is found in Acts 13:1-3, where the leaders of the church in Antioch were attentive to the Holy Spirit's guidance:

"Now in the church at Antioch there were prophets and teachers: Barnabas, Simeon called Niger, Lucius of Cyrene, Manaen (who had been brought up with Herod the tetrarch) and Saul. While they were worshiping the Lord and fasting, the Holy Spirit said, 'Set apart for me Barnabas and Saul for the work to which I have called them.' So after they had fasted and prayed, they placed their hands on them and sent them off."

This passage shows leaders in the early church who were actively worshiping and fasting when the Holy Spirit spoke to them, instructing them to set apart Barnabas and Saul (later known as the Apostle Paul) for a specific ministry. These leaders responded by praying, fasting, and obeying the guidance of the Holy Spirit, sending Barnabas and Saul on their missionary journey.

It exemplifies leaders who were sensitive and responsive to the leading of the Holy Spirit in their decisions and actions within the church.

In different churches I've been part of, there were instances where if you mentioned that God spoke to you, some Pastors might dismiss it or make you feel like an outcast. In this particular church, the leader was extraordinary. He was so open to the Holy Spirit, and I learned a lot about responding to the Holy Spirit's voice in that church. The Pastor was humble and genuine, and I can't say anything against him. He taught me that everyone in the church, not just the Pastor, can hear God's voice.

I remember one remarkable Sunday in that church. I found myself speaking God's message to the congregation unexpectedly. As soon as I took the microphone, it felt like heaven's gates opened above me, and the words I spoke weren't my own—they were God's words flowing through me. People responded, coming forward to repent and accept

Christ. It was a pivotal moment for me, surrendering to God's will completely.

This church inspired me to follow God's voice earnestly. However, despite feeling at home there, I sensed God telling me it was time to move on. I resisted this prompting for months, grappling with the idea of leaving. I was conflicted about abandoning a place where I was actively serving God. But one day, while heading home from work, I felt a strong conviction that I shouldn't attend church that evening. I shared this with my husband, and although he was upset, I chose not to go against what I believed was God's direction.

This experience taught me that God sometimes leads us out of our comfort zones for a purpose. I eventually moved to another church, but after that incident, I resolved not to make any moves without hearing clearly from God.

Your journey might differ from mine, but God walks alongside us, having a unique plan for each of us. The experience I had; God has been using it not just in my workplace but also in my neighbourhood. Everywhere I go, God works through me to touch lives—all because I obeyed God's voice when He directed me to specific areas. Even though I hesitated and didn't want to go initially, I've been a channel for God's work, impacting people's lives up to this day. It's as if wherever I am, God's presence effortlessly flows through me.

However, in some places I've been, they restrict the use of spiritual gifts. They insist that only Pastors or designated teams can minister. If they see you engaging with someone, using your spiritual gifts, it offends them. They perceive you as a rebel. This limits the manifestation of God's power in our community and generation. Many individuals are held back in their spiritual growth. Leaders must learn to hear from God and recognise the potential in their members. Sadly, some leaders close themselves off from God's direction, which restricts the lives of their congregation. Members need to be liberated. Regardless of the size of their gifts, God can magnify their impact.

Unveiling Limitations on God's Power in the Church

Leaders within the church often tend to confine the unlimited power of God once they step into their Pastoral roles. This restriction hinders God's boundless potential in the lives of people, leading to widespread frustration and disillusionment. Many individuals grow weary of the ongoing battles and restrictions in churches. I recall a person who expressed her desire to sing in church, only to be told by the Pastor that she would have to wait four years. This kind of limitation bewilders the heart that feels the Divine call.

God continuously calls upon people, yet some Pastors fail to encourage the development of their members' gifts. I remember an incident in another church where God desired to manifest His power through me to heal someone. As I prayed for the person, they were miraculously touched, but this act was met with scepticism and jealousy from the Pastoral team. They questioned my role and halted the Divine movement out of insecurity.

It is disheartening to witness how jealousy and self-interest often obstruct the work of God in churches. There have been occasions when people sought me out for prayer rather than approaching the Pastors. This predicament calls for fervent prayers—prayers for the ears and eyes of the Pastors and leaders to be opened. Many individuals remain locked in spiritual stagnation due to the ignorance and ego of those in leadership positions.

The renowned author John C. Maxwell once said, "Any success without a successor is a failure." This sentiment rings true in churches. If we intend to truly serve our church members, we must enable and uplift them to their fullest potential. Members should not merely contribute financially; they should be encouraged to use their God-given gifts. We need collective prayer—our leaders must be enlightened, and our members need guidance to recognise where they can truly flourish. Many individuals have settled in churches for decades, believing that their present location is their final destination. May the Lord open the eyes of both our leaders and members to see beyond these limitations and into the full potential of God's purpose for their lives.

Chapter 5

Control in the Church

The biblical passage, *"Upon this rock, I will build my church"* (Matthew 16:18), illustrates a foundational truth about the church—it is established by Christ Himself. This verse signifies that the church belongs to the Lord, founded upon the rock of faith in Jesus Christ. Often, however, the dynamics within churches may deviate from this fundamental principle, with some Pastors assuming excessive control and authority, treating the church as if it were their personal property.

The church, depicted as the bride of Christ, embodies a profound spiritual relationship between Christ and His followers. As such, its governance and direction should reflect Christ's intentions rather than individual authority figures. When leaders comprehend and genuinely acknowledge that the church ultimately belongs to the Lord, it catalyses a transformative shift in their approach.

Recognising the Divine ownership of the church encourages humility and a deep sense of responsibility among leaders. It fosters a mindset where leaders act as stewards rather than proprietors. This shift enables a more collaborative and inclusive approach to decision-making, incorporating the perspectives and contributions of the church body.

Leaders who acknowledge the church's belonging to Christ prioritise its spiritual health, unity, and growth rather than exerting control for personal gain. They embrace servant leadership, following Jesus's example of selflessness, sacrificial love, and nurturing the spiritual well-being of the congregation.

Furthermore, understanding that the church is Christ's bride emphasises the need for leaders to honour and cherish the church community. It promotes an environment where the congregation feels valued, heard, and encouraged to actively participate in the church's mission and ministry.

When leaders adopt this perspective, the church becomes a better place. It cultivates an atmosphere of mutual respect, encouragement, and spiritual growth. The congregation feels a sense of ownership and belonging, fostering a more vibrant and spiritually enriching community centred on Christ's teachings and example.

Jesus Example

Jesus did not control His followers, He led them. The church is currently veering off course from its mission due to overbearing and controlling leadership. This deviation undermines the essence and purpose of the church. Jesus Christ, as the builder of the church, exemplified leadership by guiding and empowering His disciples. Instead of wielding control, He led and guided people, allowing them the freedom to make choices and grow.

This contrast between leading and controlling is vital. Jesus did not impose strict control over His followers; rather, He offered guidance, wisdom, and encouragement. He allowed individuals to learn, question, and ultimately follow their own spiritual paths while offering His teachings as a foundation.

Leaders in the church today should emulate this leadership style. Rather than enforcing strict control, they should prioritise leading, guiding, and empowering individuals within the congregation. By nurturing spiritual growth, encouraging questions, and respecting individual journeys, leaders can create a more inclusive, vibrant, and spiritually enriching community aligned with the mission of the church.

Excessive Control

In the 1990s, I briefly attended a church upon my husband's sister's insistence. Arriving there, I noticed members queuing to meet the Pastor for guidance. I was raised to communicate directly with God rather than relying on Pastors for every issue.

However, the church set up cell groups and assigned leaders to new members, which seemed fine at first. Later I noticed a disturbing pattern.

After attending a Morris Cerullo meeting in Birmingham, I returned home to find the Pastors keen on controlling where we had been. They even took my tapes to examine their content. Soon, I was summoned to see the Pastor. Many waited their turn, seeking advice on matters as simple as choosing a university or career path. The Pastor asserted authority over their decisions, emphasising the need for church approval before any actions.

It struck me that members required permission for even trivial matters. The Pastor monitored their movements, dictating where they could go and what they could listen to. They even restricted access to events like revivals or conferences. This control overstepped boundaries, and I felt disheartened witnessing members' freedom curtailed in such a manner.

The church's rigorous monitoring of its members, even down to their wedding attire and personal choices, seemed excessive. Rather than fostering spiritual growth, this control stifled individual expression and independence. It saddened me to witness the absence of genuine prayer and Bible study, overshadowed by the need for constant approval and supervision from the leadership. Members were unable to freely express themselves or seek spiritual guidance beyond what was approved by the church.

This experience left a deep impression on me, highlighting the stark contrast between controlling leadership and the true essence of spiritual guidance and freedom in one's relationship with God.

When individuals are called into ministry, it's

disheartening to witness the dominance and control exhibited by some leaders. Instead of guiding, praying, and seeking Divine direction, they dictate where people can or cannot go, restricting their movement. Today, many members within the Body of Christ are losing their individuality and becoming zombies in their own churches.

My prayer is for God to open the eyes of both leaders and members to His purpose. We hold the Bible in our hands, and the Holy Spirit dwells within us. We need leaders who provide guidance without suffocating control, allowing members the freedom to move forward without having to constantly seek approval. I've heard of leaders leaving such controlling churches, and it makes me wonder how long people can be trapped in such environments. We are here for a limited time, and spending decades under control stifles the light of

God's work in our communities. It's crucial for leaders to empower and release their members, enabling them to develop and shine as representatives of Jesus in our society, rather than being mere objects of manipulation and control.

Financial Manipulation

Financial control is sadly prevalent within churches. Many individuals have been coerced financially in the name of God's provision. When I first began my Christian journey in London, people were urged to believe God for money within the church, emphasising that God is a provider. It's true that God supplies for the needs aligned with His call, yet this understanding has been twisted.

I recall attending a conference where a man of God spoke casually about financial needs without truly understanding the congregation's struggles. I felt prompted by the Holy Spirit to pray for him, to help him see the hardships faced by these people. I prayed for God to touch his heart, to open his eyes to the genuine needs of those he was asking money from. Eventually, by the next day, the man of God came back and changed his approach, acknowledging the situation and requesting money without applying undue pressure.

However, such incidents are frequent in churches, where there's a constant emphasis on financial demands. The constant collection of money during services has drained many within the Body of Christ. It's essential for the Holy Spirit to raise up individuals who understand true ministry and compassionately serve without exploiting the financial vulnerabilities of others. We must pray for our leaders to be attuned to God's leading, especially when it comes to financial matters within the church.

Back in the 80s, attending church wasn't centred around money but focused on prayer. The Pastors and leaders were looked up to for spiritual guidance, not financial demands. However, as time passed, around the late 90s, it seemed like a shift occurred—where greed and the spirit of Mammon infiltrated the church. It appeared as if Pastors were pre-planning strategies to acquire money from congregants, turning the emphasis from spiritual growth to calculated financial requests.

The essence of church gatherings today seems often overshadowed by monetary matters. Many churchgoers are increasingly reluctant to attend due to the prevalent focus on money. Members express discontent, openly expressing their dissatisfaction with the money-centric approach. This shift is a stark contrast to the primary purpose of churches, which should be to save souls, inspire and uplift, and foster growth within the kingdom of God.

Sadly, numerous churches are closing their doors, not due to God's inability to provide, but because of greed and control that have driven people away. There's a pervasive pressure on congregants to pay money, making it seem like the essence of church revolves around finances rather than Christ. As a result, many young individuals have left, while older members depart without utilising the gifts God has bestowed upon them. There's a lack of platform or opportunity for congregation members to contribute, as ministries and decisions are often confined to a select few rather than being inclusive of the entire body of Christ. This raises concerns about the future direction of the church and where it will stand in the coming years.

In today's churches, there's a noticeable shift in people's attitudes toward giving money. The congregants have become wiser in how they contribute compared to years ago. Churches receive substantial funds, but it's never deemed enough. It feels as if there's a strategic plan in place—certain tactics to encourage more monetary offerings. This approach, mainly focusing on offerings, tithes, and financial pressure, diminishes the joy of worship.

Throughout my life spent in church, I've observed Pastors and leaders who were content, not seeking lavish possessions. Their sole aim was to please God. There's a need for our leaders to realign themselves with God's principles. Having money isn't inherently wrong, but when it causes harm to the congregation, it transforms into cursed money. Members are struggling to meet basic needs, sacrificing their essential expenses to contribute to the church, causing immense suffering.

We must restore compassion for the people we lead. This wasn't the essence of Christ's teachings. Jesus provided for His disciples' needs without subjecting them to unnecessary hardship. Our God is sufficient, able to fulfil what He has called us to do. There's no need for manipulation or false promises that exploit the generosity of congregants.

To stay on mission, leaders should guide with compassion and adherence to biblical principles, considering the welfare of the congregation rather than fostering financial pressure and distress among the members.

Chapter 6

Leadership in the Church

Did you know that every church leader will be held accountable for the souls under their care? The responsibility of leadership in the church is immense! It demands wisdom, integrity, and exemplary guidance. Here is what the Bible says: Hebrews 13:17 *"Obey them that have the rule over you, and submit yourselves: for they watch for your souls, as they that must give account, that they may do it with joy, and not with grief: for that is unprofitable for you."*

Pastors and leaders must acknowledge that it is God who has granted them the privilege to use their gifts and lead. When they begin, they should recognise that they were once ordinary individuals in the church, and God bestowed upon them grace to serve under someone else's guidance. To step into their ministry and gain trust, they also need to trust others, including our mentors.

It's not merely about joining a church to work towards fulfilling personal destinies. As leaders, our aim should be to guide and empower people to fulfil their destinies. Our destiny becomes intertwined with theirs, recognising that those fulfilling our destiny have their own paths to fulfil.

Having a strategic plan is crucial. As leaders, it's our responsibility. If we fail to release individuals into their destinies, we fall short, regardless of our authority. We would be failing against God's grace, as mentioned in Ephesians 4.

Ephesians 4:11 says "*And he gave some, apostles; and some, prophets; and some, evangelists; and some, Pastors and teachers.*"

This verse describes the various roles or gifts given by God to individuals within the church, including Pastors and teachers, among others. Apostolic leaders, as mentioned in verse 11, were given by God to the church. He generously gave these diverse gifts to elevate and guide individuals in their roles, establishing order within the church. All these gifts exist today because God entrusted them to the church, of which we are a part.

If we choose to hoard our gifts or hinder others from serving beyond just aiding us, we are essentially failing God, who entrusted us with these gifts. It's a sinful act since God granted these gifts to mentor and contribute to the church. Apostles, Pastors, teachers, and other ordered gifts are intended to perfect and edify the church.

As a Pastor, if you're merely safeguarding your gift and preventing others from rising up, you're not serving God's purpose. You're neglecting the responsibility God has given you and jeopardising the grace bestowed upon you. Remember, God can withdraw His grace.

There are many Pastors among a vast array of people in the church, each with distinct roles and responsibilities guided by God's intentions.

I've observed some Pastors I've known for decades and they're no longer where they used to be. Today, we stand where they once stood, as God utilises someone who has been released to use their gifting. When you are elevated, it's not because you own the power or gift; rather, it flows from heaven to you. However, if God sees that you aren't using it according to His plan, He has the authority to halt it. The Holy Spirit, being from heaven, is beyond our control.

Some Pastor-leaders I encountered failed to release others, and as a consequence, their lives concluded without a successor. They prioritised their family over raising successors. Even if they had children, not all were equipped to continue the work. Remember, it's God who empowers us to build an army for His purpose. We are part of God's army, and He sends us to train others. However, some focus solely on their legacy, wanting their family to reign for years. Sadly, many lose their anointing before their demise. Starting well and finishing well is crucial for any Pastor or leader.

The anointing upon you is not yours to possess; it can be transferred. God never withdraws His anointing, but we risk losing it when we become proud and believe we control it. It's ungodly to hinder other Pastors doing God's work due to jealousy. Jealousy is a tool of the devil, not of God.

Jealousy and hatred are tools Satan uses to sow destruction and confusion within the church. Dear brothers and sisters, let us fix our eyes on God, the giver of gifts, so that we may raise a multitude for His kingdom. In this earthly realm, an army doesn't harbour jealousy among its ranks; rather, each knows their role and promotes one another as they fulfil their duties seamlessly.

I've witnessed Pastors displaying jealousy toward the gifts of others. However, it's vital to acknowledge that these gifts are from God. Our focus should be finding our place in God's kingdom, not on personal accomplishments. The bestowing of gifts isn't a reward for merit; it's a manifestation of God's grace upon an individual. Let's celebrate the grace of God in each other. When we honour the work God does through others, it doesn't diminish our own ministry. Just because something hasn't occurred in our ministry doesn't mean it won't happen when your time has come.

I've witnessed numerous instances of jealousy and hatred hindering the expression of others' gifts. When God intends to reveal His blessings through someone, some rush to pray against these Divine endowments. Are we serving God or aligning ourselves with the schemes of Satan?

Reflecting on my years in the church, I've often lamented seeing jealousy disrupt the multiplication of God's gifts meant to reach and benefit others. As a person who values peace and love, I rejoice in seeing God's gifts multiply to bless and serve more people. Our goal is to glorify Jesus Christ, not ourselves. It's through His name that demons are cast out, and the sick are healed, bringing glory to God.

Unfortunately, I've witnessed instances where individuals withhold glory from others within the church. This behaviour is unrighteous and wicked. We must pray for Pastors and church leaders not to impede the work of God. Instead, may they embody and showcase God's glory. It's time for the Church and individuals to embrace and utilise their gifts. These gifts, freely given by God, come at a personal cost for the individual receiving them. Let us not quench these gifts or allow the enemy to use us against each other.

May the Lord bless our church and grant us growth and multiplication, not merely in numbers but for the expansion of His kingdom. Our faith's completion rests with God, the Alpha and Omega, the beginning and the end. Our time in this world is brief; we age, losing the youthful vigour we once had.

It saddens me to witness individuals who've spent years in Bible school or training yet haven't realised their potential. It's essential to encourage and enable everyone to develop their God-given gifts. Many yearn to contribute but lack the opportunity or support. God desires each person to manifest their gifts.

We must create avenues for people to use their talents, nurturing, and praying for them. Mere recruitment into our church isn't enough; everyone present has a Divine purpose. If after several decades, individuals show no growth or have no successors, it questions our leadership and Pastoral guidance.

The kingdom of God needs expansion. While some of us grow older, others grow younger in their faith journey. We, as leaders, must align ourselves with God's purpose, not our own. We shouldn't limit others but empower and release them. Even when they leave our fold, they remain connected to us as spiritual children, contributing to different ministries.

Let us embrace a culture of support, enabling the growth of individuals, and fostering a network of relationships that transcends mere church affiliations.

Prayer For The Church Leader

Heavenly Father,

We come before You today with hearts full of gratitude for the gift of our Pastor. We thank You for the wisdom, compassion, and dedication they bring to our congregation. We lift them up to You, acknowledging the weight of responsibility and challenges they face daily.

Grant our Pastor strength, Lord, both in mind and body. May Your Divine guidance be their compass as they lead and shepherd Your flock. Bless them with discernment in decision-making, clarity in vision, and wisdom in their teachings.

Cover our Pastor with Your protection, shielding them from the arrows of doubt, criticism, and spiritual warfare. Pour out Your peace upon them in moments of uncertainty and grant them courage to stand firm in faith.

We ask for a refreshing of their spirit, Lord. Renew their passion for Your word and for ministering to others. Fill them afresh with Your anointing and empower them with Your Holy Spirit to continue their Divine calling.

May You bless their family, Lord, for the sacrifices they make and the support they offer. Strengthen their relationships and bring harmony within their home.

Father, we pray for physical and emotional rejuvenation for our Pastor. Surround them with a community that supports, uplifts, and appreciates their efforts.

We thank You, Lord, for the blessings our Pastor brings into our lives. Grant them joy in their service and continue to use them mightily for Your glory.

In Jesus' name, we pray. Amen.

Chapter 7

Choosing a Healthy Church

A healthy church is one where leaders listen to God, understand His voice, and allow people to use their gifts. Let's get this straight. The church is not the Pastor; the church is us, the members. The church is not a building; the church is us, the body. A healthy church is centered on the Bible. It teaches and preaches God's Word, guiding its members to understand and apply the Scriptures in their daily lives. A healthy church fosters an environment that promotes spiritual growth and maturity. It provides opportunities for discipleship, learning, and personal development in faith.

Healthy churches have strong, godly leadership that guides the congregation, provides Pastoral care, and leads by example. There is also a system of accountability in place to ensure integrity and transparency. Ultimately, a healthy church places Jesus Christ at the center of everything it does. It seeks to glorify God, follow Christ's teachings, and reflect His love to the world.

In contrast, an unhealthy church is controlled by a leader or a team who limits others from using their gifts, only recognising those they personally anoint. In a healthy assembly, those in leadership mentor and encourage those coming after them, preparing them for leadership roles.

When a church doesn't permit the expression of individual gifts or stifles growth, it's better to leave. Staying in such an environment limits personal development and hinders the use of one's God-given abilities. Seeking God's guidance through prayer is vital to discern whether a church is the right fit. A church solely focused on financial contributions without regard for its members' spiritual growth and well-being is not a place for your calling.

A verse that reflects the concept of using one's gifts and talents within the context of the church is found in 1 Peter 4:10

"As every man hath received the gift, even so minister the same one to another, as good stewards of the manifold grace of God."

This verse emphasises using the gifts received from God to serve others within the church, highlighting the importance of contributing to the community of believers through the unique abilities and talents each individual possesses.

The Church's Mission: Equipping, Serving, and Unifying Believers.

Ephesians speaks to a critical mission of the church, underlining its purpose for the equipping and edification of believers.

Ephesians 4:12-13 *"For the perfecting of the saints, for the work of the ministry, for the edifying of the body of Christ: Till we all come in the unity of the faith, and of the knowledge of the Son of God, unto a perfect man, unto the measure of the stature of the fullness of Christ."*

This passage underscores several key points regarding the role and mission of the church:

1. **Perfecting of the Saints:** The church is responsible for nurturing and maturing

believers in their faith. It's a place where individuals are equipped, strengthened, and guided to grow spiritually, morally, and emotionally in their Christian journey.

2. **Work of the Ministry:** The church isn't just a place to attend but a body actively involved in the work of spreading the Gospel, serving others, and ministering to both the spiritual and practical needs of the community. It's about living out the love of Christ in action.

3. **Edifying the Body of Christ:** Building up and strengthening the community of believers is crucial. The church serves as a supportive and nurturing environment where individuals encourage, support, and uplift one another.

The verse goes on to emphasise the desired

outcome of these efforts: unity in faith and knowledge of Christ. This unity doesn't mean uniformity but a shared understanding of fundamental truths and a growing intimacy with Jesus Christ. It's a unity that transcends cultural, social, and personal differences, binding believers together in love and purpose.

However, many churches have missed the mark by focusing more on activities, rituals, or programs without nurturing genuine spiritual growth. Some may prioritise tradition or rituals over the development of believers. In such cases, the primary mission of spiritual growth, community building, and active ministry might take a back seat.

A healthy church, aligned with the mission in Ephesians 4:12-13, spotlights spiritual growth, empowers its members for service, fosters a supportive community, and focuses on unity rooted in faith and understanding of Christ. When these elements are emphasised, the church becomes a vibrant and impactful force, fulfilling its mission as intended by God.

If you find yourself in an unhealthy church environment, there might be a lack of appreciation for diverse gifts or a genuine purpose to equip and support those who come after them. It's advisable for both members and leaders to seek guidance and move on to a place where God is at the helm. A church where God's influence prevails, not where a Pastor dominates and controls, is the right place to be. Staying in such an environment can lead to stagnation and lack of growth. It's essential to seek a place where your gifts can flourish. Merely attending, paying tithes, and offerings without growth isn't what God intended for us. Productive churches foster an atmosphere where people support and groom future leaders.

Sometimes, when a church opens opportunities for you to use your gifts and notices that you may excel beyond their understanding or surpass their leadership, instead of embracing and supporting you, they may turn against you. I've witnessed this happen. They'll suddenly oppose you. In such instances, it's crucial to turn to God, seeking His guidance and protection. If God directs you to a specific church, He will safeguard you, even during challenging times. I urge people to rise above this. God calls each one of us to a victorious place. Time is passing, slipping away, and darkness is looming.

Many churches are merely going through the motions of religion. Our possessions in this world won't accompany us, but our priority should be pleasing our Master, not ourselves, not our egos, nor our Pastors. Our purpose is to please the Lord, to be attentive to His voice daily. As a member, without sensitivity to God's voice, discerning the next steps becomes challenging. Our feet must move in line with God's purpose for us. Every individual has a God-given purpose, a destiny to fulfil. If you realise your church inhibits your fulfilment, I encourage my brothers and sisters to seek God's guidance to connect with someone who can aid them. Sometimes, this decision brings tears, but it's a choice worth making.

There's no easy way to leave a church where you've been deeply hurt or where your potential has been stifled for years. Perhaps you aren't even aware of your own gifts anymore. These gifts lay dormant, untouched, and the church denies you the opportunity to utilise them. If you desire to partake in evangelism, but it doesn't align with their preferences, they obstruct you. Personally, I experienced this blockage; someone even prophesied negatively against my efforts, praying for its failure. There are countless others like me, even older, who've left churches or passed away without fulfilling their purposes.

Church Arise!

It's time for the Church to awaken; it's time for the members to rise. This is a call to the Body of Christ to embrace their true calling on Earth. We have one chance in this life; it's a singular journey. We ought to pray for our Pastors and leaders, as many of them will have to answer to God in heaven. If they remain obstinate and refuse change, remember, it's not about material wealth – not about money, luxurious houses, or fancy cars. It's about purpose; it's about liberating people to fulfil their destinies. Ephesians chapters one through six explain how Paul, an ordinary man, was used mightily.

Paul was an ordinary man, going about his business until God called him in the book of Acts. At that point, he didn't know anything about Jesus or preaching the gospel. When Jesus encountered him, He seized Paul, temporarily blinded him, and directed him to someone who could lead him and impart knowledge about Himself. Jesus didn't just leave Paul in the church to follow others; He guided him into the hands of someone who was already part of the fold, providing instructions. This is how the members should be handled by Pastors and leaders. I'm addressing leaders and Pastors—it's time for change. The current approach isn't what God desires. Every church member should have an active role to play so that together, we can impact nations. Presently, nations remain untouched, and it's time for a shift.

It was a very painful experience for me. The day I decided to explore my area and be productive was the day my struggles began within my church. Despite leaving the place for over three years, they kept sending people to me, feigning ignorance as if they weren't aware. This is not in alignment with God's happiness. I spent fourteen long years there, and they still persistently pursued my return, offering me leadership positions. However, they were oblivious to my gifts and calling—what God has intended for me seemed unimportant to them. Why should I subject myself to such oppression?

Many individuals, like me, find themselves in the church, faithfully participating in offerings and tithes, to the point where they are regularly addressed as 'faithful servants.' However, the church confines them to a perpetual role of servitude, hindering them from fulfilling their purpose. The church needs to wake up; Jesus is calling people to a greater purpose. Things cannot continue as they are. We require individuals filled with the Holy Spirit.

I recall a man of God who passed away and didn't raise anyone else but his own son to take over. He neglected others in the ministry. Although the ministry was substantial when he passed, it seemed as if the ministry died with him, rather than nurturing and elevating others who possessed various gifts. Instead, they suppressed those gifts. They went as far as praying against individuals who felt called by God, acting as if they alone had the authority to do so. This ignorance is prevalent in the body of Christ. May the Lord, save us from such practices.

Five Steps to Choose a Healthy Church

1. **Pray for Guidance:** Seek God's guidance and pray for wisdom in choosing a church. Ask for discernment to find a community aligned with your spiritual needs and beliefs.

2. **Visit Various Churches:** Attend different churches to get a feel for their worship style, teaching, and community. This exploration can help you identify what resonates with you spiritually.

3. **Check for Involvement:** Look for opportunities to get involved. A healthy church encourages involvement in various ministries and activities that match your interests and spiritual gifts.

4. **Meet Church Leadership:** Get to know the church leaders and their vision and

mission for the church. Understand their approach to leadership and ministry before commitment.

5. **Trust The Holy Spirit Voice Within:** Ultimately, trust your instincts and the leading of the Holy Spirit. Choose a church where you feel spiritually nourished, connected, and where you can grow, contribute meaningfully and walk in purpose.

Remember, finding a healthy church might take time. Don't rush the decision, seek counsel, and trust God to guide you to the community where you can grow spiritually and serve others effectively.

Chapter 8

Exposing Lies in the Church

A few years back, we experienced something quite baffling when our Pastor stood on the platform and made an announcement. It was about unlocking our destinies, allowing us to step into what God had called us to do. Eager and prepared, we embarked on a course that was said to be the missing link in our training, only to discover it was a duplicate of what we'd already undergone. A costly £300 'additional' course, promised certificates that never materialised. It left us disillusioned, scratching our heads in confusion.

We held our church leaders in high esteem, looking up to them for guidance and spiritual direction. But this incident shattered our trust. The highest levels of the church were partaking in such deceit. It was disheartening. Slowly, one after another, people started drifting away from the church. There was a shift in the atmosphere, a waning of faith in the leadership that had once inspired us.

As we drew closer to the inner workings of the church, we witnessed many falsehoods and manipulations. They would articulate one thing but fail to execute it. In any other scenario, this would be deemed illegal—like a consumer issue when a purchased product doesn't serve its purpose. But within the church, we tend to overlook it, attributing everything to God. We kept our focus on Jesus, yet the turmoil within the church persisted.

The reality is, there's an array of lies and injustices happening in churches, with members continuing to contribute financially without knowing where their funds are truly going. Only God can defend the members against such practices. It's a stark reminder that despite the disillusionment, we must seek God's guidance and discernment to navigate such challenges within our faith communities.

The Father Of Lies

"Ye are of your father the devil, and the lusts of your father ye will do. He was a murderer from the beginning,

and abode not in the truth, because there is no truth in him. When he speaketh a lie, he speaketh of his own: for he is a liar, and the father of it." John 8:44

In the verse above, Jesus identifies the devil as the father of lies. When church leaders exhibit deceitful behaviour or propagate falsehoods, it raises a significant concern as it contradicts the very essence of truth that Jesus embodies and encourages in his teachings.

The analogy drawn by Jesus about the devil being the father of lies implies that falsehood and deception are intrinsic to the devil's character. Therefore, when individuals, especially those in positions of spiritual leadership within a church, engage in deceitful conduct or propagate untruths, it stands in direct contradiction to the teachings of Christ.

Church leaders are expected to embody and

advocate for truthfulness, integrity, and honesty, reflecting the character of Christ. When they deviate from this standard by habitually lying or promoting falsehoods, it raises doubts about their spiritual alignment and the authenticity of their leadership.

Such behaviour not only contradicts the teachings of Jesus but also undermines the trust and credibility that congregants place in their spiritual leaders. It's a departure from the qualities expected of those entrusted with guiding and nurturing a congregation in the ways of faith, truth, and righteousness.

Therefore, the verse suggests that leaders who persistently engage in falsehoods are not aligning themselves with the principles of truth and integrity espoused by Christ. Instead, their actions may reflect an allegiance to deceit and untruthfulness, characteristics that align with the nature of the father of lies—the devil.

Lies From The Pulpit

It's essential for us, as a church, to pray earnestly for our leaders. There's an urgent need to rekindle a spirit of humility and compassion within their hearts. The creeping influence of greed has disrupted the core values of our church. It's distressing to see that our leaders seem indifferent to the struggles of the congregation, prioritising their own needs above all else.

It's important to note that these observations don't apply to every leader, but regrettably, they are reflective of certain individuals within the church.

There's a noticeable contradiction between their teachings about walking by faith and the pressure they exert on us to give offerings. It feels like a demonstration of their lack of belief in God's provision unless they manipulate the congregation into giving money. This confusion and deception have become pervasive within the church.

Every preacher who steps onto the platform seems driven to raise offerings. It's disheartening to hear them claim that God told them specific amounts to ask for, only to change the numbers later. This constant focus on monetary figures seems contrary to the true nature of God, who is simple and abundant in provision. It's unsettling to witness this change in approach over the years.

In the past, there used to be an emphasis on prayer before offering, allowing individuals to discern what they could give. But now, it feels like a series of falsehoods dominating the process. God isn't about constantly changing demands for pounds or dollars; He's about providing and teaching us to trust Him. The teachings seem to have deviated from their original intent, and there's a pressing need to return to the genuine essence of faith and trust in God's provision.

Exposing The Offering Lies

There are a lot of lies in every preaching; every person who steps onto the platform to preach is expected to raise an offering. This can't be the voice of God. You come to the platform claiming 'God told me somebody can give £1000,' and later 'God says if you have £500.' Then, if they don't come out or a few respond, it's reduced to £200. Saying 'God is changing his mind' too often makes it all seem insincere. We have listened to this for decades but our eyes are now open; we know that God doesn't change. He doesn't consistently communicate in terms of pounds or dollars. There's too much emphasis on this.

I remember two ladies from my church, one of them was a single parent relying on government aid to survive. Then, another Preacher from America came to the platform stating that God wanted to make some people millionaires if they could give £2000. People rushed forward hoping to become millionaires, but none of their situations changed. If God truly wants to make someone a millionaire, He can do it without requiring a specific amount.

The spirit of Mammon has gripped some leaders, causing them to overlook the struggles of the members. It appears they are driven by greed or lack of belief, which contradicts what they teach us. When we share our problems, they tell us to trust God, but when it comes to money, there are all sorts of gimmicks and promises. It's disheartening because it seems like their primary focus is on taking as much as they can, and there is a noticeable absence of love in the hearts of our leaders.

Compassion Has Been Lost

Where is the love? There seems to be no love in the hearts of many of our leaders towards the members; instead, they prioritise what they can gain from them. Many members spend their time volunteering without pay. In on church, the ushers who were busy working during the service were not given free sermon recording to listen to at home considering their busy schedules. This particular church demanded payment for it. God represents knowledge and compassion, yet there's no compassion shown towards the church members. It's all about grabbing more, while leaders receive salaries and church members struggle.

One of the prominent verses in the Bible reflecting Jesus's compassion is Matthew 14:14.

"And Jesus went forth, and saw a great multitude, and was moved with compassion toward them, and he healed their sick."

This verse illustrates how Jesus responded to the needs of the people, moved by compassion, and healed those who were sick. It exemplifies His caring nature and willingness to help those in distress. Has the church lost the heart of compassion?

We need to pray for the church because it's sick. Manipulation of members is rampant. Leaders often show no support when members face problems, especially in larger churches where they have little time for people. I recall a friend seeking a reference letter from a Christian church and being asked for a reference from their own church. Shockingly, they were denied the reference simply because they lacked an offering or tithes card, emphasising how it's all about money and personal gain. If you don't comply with their demands, you receive nothing in return.

When those who are meant to heal the sick within the church find themselves ailing, it raises the question: how can the church itself be healed? If those tasked with healing the sick are now in need of healing, may the Lord restore the health of our leaders and instill in them a renewed reverence for God. May the Lord empower our leaders and help us. The church members also need to wake up and keep their eyes open.

I recall a lady from our church more than twenty years ago. At that time, the Pastor, now a significant figure in the ministry, asked her to help him find a wife. She suggested her sister from their home country, and they connected. They got married, and the sister assisted with wedding arrangements, sending money and gifts. Yet, when the Pastor and his wife returned to London, there were struggles with obtaining the wife's visa. He urged the sister to vouch for her, emphasising their relationship.

However, once the wife arrived, things changed drastically. The Pastor turned against the sister who had introduced them. He spread lies about her in Nigeria and within the church community. This was deeply hurtful, causing a twenty year rift where they ceased any contact. It's perplexing how a respected church leader, a Bible scholar, could behave in such a manner.

Today, he remains a prominent figure in the ministry, still preaching the gospel. It raises questions about the authenticity of the gospel preached by such individuals. This behaviour, deeply troubling, necessitates addressing by the Holy Spirit within the body of Christ. It's a prayerful hope that such leaders open their eyes and ears, avoiding a fate unworthy of heaven due to the harm caused by spreading falsehoods and hurting others.

I recall another church I attended where the Pastor was deceiving the congregation by spreading lies about the committee, claiming they hadn't compensated him for his services. This falsehood stirred up anger and conflict within the congregation, leading the members to give money to the Pastor under false pretences. It's disheartening to witness a Pastor, a learned Bible scholar, resorting to such deceit for personal gain.

Where has the fear of God vanished in the hearts of our church leaders? May the Lord intervene and restore integrity and honesty in our church leadership.

Lord Wash Your Church

Lord, cleanse your church. Lord, restore your church to its original mission. There is an absence of godly reverence in our leaders, a void where love should reside in their hearts. How can they bring about spiritual transformation? How can we expect the power of God to manifest in our church when the leaders perpetuate continual lies year after year?

Dear Lord, help your church in confronting these prevalent lies that permeate through our pulpits. They claim Divine messages that were never spoken, sowing discord within families, yet they claim to be scholars of the Bible. This isn't a matter of ignorance; it's a disconnection from the Holy Spirit. If they were truly filled with the Holy Spirit, it would be inconceivable for them to propagate falsehoods knowingly.

Lord, grant mercy upon our leaders. Help them

recognise their wrongdoings and lead them back to the true path of spiritual integrity. Amen.

Chapter 9

A Church With Power

God is in the process of rebuilding and raising a Church that will once again walk in Divine power. This Church mirrors the experiences of the day of Pentecost, where the power of God was vividly manifested. It's a Church where the Word of God is proclaimed with power, accompanied by wonders and demonstrations of the Holy Spirit. Acts 1:8 speaks of this power being conferred upon believers.

In Acts, the initial Church journeyed to Jerusalem, awaiting the promise of God. They were not seeking merely the gift of tongues but patiently waiting for God's promise to be fulfilled. The power of God descended upon them on the day of Pentecost. This outpouring transformed individuals like Peter, who, once fearful and denying Jesus, became bold for the Lord. Peter and John encountered a man at the gate called Beautiful and declared, 'Silver and gold I do not have, but what I do have I give you: In the name of Jesus Christ of Nazareth, rise up and walk.'

The Church empowered by God is one marked by unity, love, and the operation of Divine power. Without the power of God, effectiveness in our ministries becomes a challenge. Sadly, this power seems to be waning in the lives of many, redirecting their focus elsewhere. If the power of God genuinely resides within, there's no inclination to use the pulpit for deceit or to devise ways to extract money from those unable to give.

And so, the spirits of greed must vacate the Church, making room for the Holy Spirit to reign supreme. As we gather in church, the focal point of our gatherings should be the power of God. Without the Holy Spirit, we cannot operate as Jesus did. Attempting to do so without Him will result in failure. In this era, for the work to progress, we desperately need the Holy Spirit; our endeavours are futile without His presence.

The Spirit of Jesus Christ needs to permeate the Pastor, the members, and every corner of the world, manifesting that Christ is alive. Unfortunately, the Church has become a subject of jest and mere conversation. This is not the Church that Jesus sacrificed Himself for; He didn't die for a feeble, weak, anaemic Church. He died for a Church filled with power, one that reflects love and genuinely cares for people. His sacrifice was to redeem and set His bride free.

For a Church to be great, it must be a reflection of Jesus Himself. Everything we've read and known about Jesus should find its place within this Church. Anything short of that is not the great Church that Jesus envisioned.

God is orchestrating the return of the prodigals to a renewed church in these last days. This Church must mirror the events of Acts Chapter Two in the upper room, where power and manifestation resonated profoundly. It's not merely about preaching; it's about demonstrating the tangible reality of God's presence. The old routine of singing 'hallelujahs' and superficial practices won't suffice to draw people back to church. Nowadays, it's challenging to draw them back unless they witness signs and wonders that prove our belief. A truly great church doesn't just speak about signs; it lives and breathes them. Our practice must align with our preaching; otherwise, the full potential of God's power will elude us. God is summoning His Church to once again exemplify Jesus in every aspect, embodying the essence of who He is.

Mark 16:17-18, states:

"And these signs shall follow them that believe; In my name shall they cast out devils; they shall speak with new tongues; They shall take up serpents; and if they drink any deadly thing, it shall not hurt them; they shall lay hands on the sick, and they shall recover."

These signs shall follow those who believe in my name; they shall cast out devils, lay hands on the sick, and they shall recover. When these signs are manifest in the church, it becomes the Great Church of God. God didn't call us to form a club or engage in debates, nor did He summon us to merely attend and daydream in church. He called us to demonstrate, to transform the church into a healing centre where people are blessed, receive their blessings, and go forth to bless others. This is the kind of church that God seeks.

A great church operates in the power of the Holy Spirit, abides by the Word of God, and doesn't just preach the gospel and then engage in slander or discourage the use of people's gifts. It's a church that mirrors Jesus' care and compassion for his disciples. Jesus, even after His resurrection, sought out His disciples, especially Thomas, to reveal Himself and confirm their faith. He didn't abandon them but continually sought them out. Similarly, the church, led by its Pastors and leaders, should encourage disciples to go out, reproduce, and spread the gospel. If a church isn't reproducing, it remains stagnant.

In reflecting on my previous church, I realised that its constant turmoil stemmed from the absence of the Word of God. Although prayer was a prominent activity, the church lacked a foundation in the Word. The adversary exploited this void, causing recurrent disturbances every few months, disrupting the church's harmony.

A great church is more than just powerful; it is imbued with love, understanding, and a practical application of the Word in everyday life. Our lives should mirror the teachings of Christ in both speech and action. We need the Lord's guidance to stand firm in support of our leaders. Many current leaders are driven solely by material gain, aspiring to grand homes, expensive cars, or even private jets. Their insatiable desires outstrip the call to seek the kingdom of heaven and His righteousness first.

When we prioritise seeking God's kingdom, everything we need is provided. There's no lack for those devoted to God, filled with His power and dedicated to prayer. A great church doesn't merely preach the Gospel; it bears the weight of its message through living it out.

Churches fixated on monetary gains often neglect the Word of God and lack practical application. They preach without practicing what they teach. Instead, let us pray for God's guidance to lead us to the church of God's choosing. We need more prayer, more Power, and more Anointing to reach our generation. Our world is filled with hurting souls, and we can't reach them unless God touches us first. We need His touch to heal and empower us, guiding our generation towards the Lord.

Chapter 10

Church Hopping

Many people wounded by church experiences, resort to "church hopping." However, there's no perfect church—only the Lord is perfect! If you're leaving a church solely due to someone's teaching or words, your spiritual growth might be hindered. Instead, consider that perfection isn't found in any church; only God is perfect. Focus on listening to the Holy Spirit rather than seeking perfection in a church setting.

"Church hopping" refers to the practice of moving from one church to another frequently or regularly, often without establishing long-term involvement or commitment to any particular congregation. This can be due to various reasons such as dissatisfaction with the church's teachings, conflicts, a search for a better fit spiritually or socially, or personal preferences.

You might find yourself thinking, "I can't find a church, what should I do?" It's beneficial to spend time in prayer at home, reading your Bible, and strengthening your connection with God. Remember, we are the Church. Sometimes, amidst our search for the right congregation, it's crucial to stay home and pray for guidance to find the right church.

It's important to pray about the Pastor of the

church you're considering attending. Ask the Lord to reveal the authenticity of the Pastor's calling because nowadays, many claim to be Pastors but may be something else. Some might lead you astray, making you reluctant to return to church. Satan often tries to imitate God's ways, so we must remain spiritually vigilant. Understanding the Word of God is essential for our lives and letting the Holy Spirit guide us in making choices. Through prayer, God speaks to us. It might take time to grow in our relationship with God before we can discern His voice. As we develop our spiritual journey, we become more attuned to hearing His guidance.

Additionally, it's vital not only to pray but also to be watchful. Scripture encourages us to respect authority, but it's equally important to discern the authenticity of that authority. Some leaders may have hidden motives or lack the Holy Spirit's guidance, but when the Spirit resides within you, you'll discern the true nature of the leadership you follow.

I recall my time in my former church, the fourth one I attended in this country. Throughout, there were troubles, yet I hesitated to leave. I felt no desire to depart until God revealed something significant to me. In a vision, I held a key, attempting to unlock the church's door, but it remained shut despite my efforts. Then, through someone sent by God, I was urged to leave with my children. I prayed and tried every means, yet the door wouldn't budge. However, in another vision, I departed and returned. This time, as I opened the door, it swung open effortlessly. Sometimes, God leads us away for a period and eventually brings us back, either to the same church or elsewhere. When we remain close to God, He communicates with us, often through various people. God's intentions are never in jest. He wants us to grow stronger in Him, espccially when faced with challenges within the church. The trials I faced strengthened me today. Had I remained in my comfort zone initially, my growth might have been hindered. You can't just church-hop, seeking a better place, for there is no perfect church. Only God is perfect. If you have a calling, God will guide you to where you need to be. My departure from the fourth church wasn't planned, but when God spoke, I had to obey. Church-hopping isn't the answer; it's about drawing closer to God.

Once you find yourself in the right place, it doesn't guarantee immunity from being hurt by someone or something within the church. If you leave a church simply because someone hurt you, it might not be a sufficient reason to depart. Make sure your departure is led by the Lord and that the next church you choose is His direction. If you keep switching churches without listening to God's guidance, you'll likely repeat the same cycle. It's essential to surrender to God's will. If you keep changing churches, your spiritual growth might stagnate. Being judgmental towards others won't help; we all come from diverse backgrounds and levels.

The key is to personally know God and seek guidance from the Holy Spirit. Without His guidance, progress in your spiritual journey might be hindered. Our ultimate rest is in Christ, not in a man or a physical church building. Accusing others of causing your downfall isn't fair; it's often our choice to fall when we put too much reliance on people instead of focusing on God. He is the ultimate finisher of our faith, not any man according to Hebrews 12:2 *"Looking unto Jesus the author and finisher of our faith; who for the joy that was set before him endured the cross, despising the shame, and is set down at the right hand of the throne of God."*

Pastors After My Heart

"And I will give you Pastors according to mine heart, which shall feed you with knowledge and understanding." Jeremiah 3:15

Despite the straying of many from their mission, God still has faithful servants on earth—Pastors chosen according to His heart. They are entrusted to feed His people with knowledge and understanding, guiding them along the right path.

Let us not create problems for ourselves by harshly judging Pastors and leaders. They are human and prone to faults. We should pray for them instead. If God indicates that a particular church is where we are meant to be, then we should remain steadfast, even if we notice imperfections in our Pastor. We must pray for their transformation and ask God to change the situation. After all, everyone, including Pastors, makes mistakes, and God's desire is for all to repent and grow. Expecting perfection from our Pastors is unrealistic; they, too, are evolving just as we are. Therefore, it's vital to allow God to work through us and help us progress. If we approach church or the Bible with a preconceived notion instead of surrendering to God, our growth will stagnate. Surrender to God's guidance, and He will lead us to a place of spiritual growth and fulfillment. If you have a Divine calling, God won't confine you to one place indefinitely. We need to pray until we are directed to a community where our calling and purpose align with God's intentions.

I earnestly encourage you to draw nearer to God, to truly understand His heart. It's my advice to those who've experienced disappointment or hurt, recognising that holding onto grievances or waiting for others to change isn't conducive to growth. Instead, allow the Lord to guide you, to teach you.

Consider this in the context of attending a church. It's crucial to attend with a purpose—to seek personal growth regardless of external circumstances. Reflecting on my own experience, I recall the initial challenges I faced when serving as an usher in my former church. Despite potential reasons to leave due to others' behaviour, I reminded myself that my purpose wasn't tied to them but to God's calling. We have limited time in this life, and it's vital not to squander it on distractions that deviate from our mission to reach those God has placed in our paths.

I recently attended another church at a friend's invitation. During discussions, many attendees shared how they discovered the church. Some sought assurance before committing, illustrating that people are actively searching for genuine spiritual connections.

Chapter 11

Knowing God

My plea is for the body of Christ to personally seek and know God.

If our familiarity lies solely with the church or the Pastor, and not with Christ Himself, we may encounter hardships at the hands of leaders. Such suffering might actually be a result of the enemy's influence. As the Bible states:

"And such as do wickedly against the covenant shall he corrupt by flatteries: but the people that do know their God shall be strong, and do exploits." Daniel 11:32

When you truly know God, it's through knowing His Word. Without understanding the Word of God, you may not truly comprehend God. The Word serves as a mirror, reflecting God's character and revealing how He operates. Any concept or belief outside the Word of God can be questioned. The Bible stresses that knowing the truth will set you free. Your liberation isn't from knowing the Pastor; it stems from grasping the truth. Jesus Christ is the truth — He proclaimed, 'Me and my Father, we are one.' This unity between Jesus and His Father, with the Holy Spirit dwelling within Jesus, elucidates the interconnectedness. The same Spirit that raised Christ from the dead resides in you.

The Holy Spirit serves as a guide to help you comprehend the Bible. When you allow it to offer understanding, it enlightens your spiritual senses. It gives you the discernment to recognise falsehoods in teachings or preaching's around you. This intelligence within us aids in steering us away from errors. By reading your Bible and fostering a genuine relationship with Jesus through prayer and communication with the Father, you gain a deep understanding of Christ. As mentioned in John 14:14, *"If you ask anything in my name, I will do it,"* Jesus' commitment is firm, and His promises to heal or fulfill are assured.

It's not solely about having a personal connection with the Pastor. Today, a Pastor may have numerous congregants to attend to, making it impossible for them to remember everything about each person. However, God knows you intimately.

He sees and recognises you wherever you are. Even before you come to Christ, He is working within your heart, prompting you towards Him. As soon as you turn to Christ, you are never alone; the Holy Spirit dwells within you. Whether you're aware or not, His presence remains, drawing you closer through prayer, communion, and seeking to know Him. Relying solely on knowing the Pastor can lead to spiritual stagnation.

You might reach a point where growth halts, despite attending church, merely seeing the Pastor and the church building without any deeper connection. When you truly know God, even amidst lies or false teachings, you discern because the Spirit of Christ, the same Spirit that raised Jesus from the dead, resides and abides within us. Therefore, it's essential to know God personally for genuine success in our Christian journey; we must seek to know Him for ourselves.

God desires to build each individual, nurturing each person as His precious child. Jesus seeks a personal relationship with us. The church isn't merely a physical structure; it's the presence of Jesus within you, fostering a deeper connection. Attending church for praise and worship aids in spiritual growth, but true understanding of Christ comes through personal revelation. Knowing God personally is essential, achieved through studying His Word, consistent prayer, and dedicating our entire lives to Him.

When we truly know God for ourselves, no one can sway us with misleading teachings because the Spirit of God guides us. We must pray fervently, seeking an intimate relationship with God daily. Yearning for His presence, we ask for His power to align with His will, to fulfil His purpose in our lives.

We plead for His deliverance, not just for ourselves but for our families, drawing nearer to God as we ask Him to draw nearer to us.

Talking to God as a father, a friend, a companion, opens our hearts to His guidance. We seek His enlightenment, asking for eyes that see, ears that hear, and a heart open to His presence. Loving God above all else, even above family and friends, aligns us with His teachings and ensures our growth in Him.

Through God's Word, we attain power. We're empowered not for our own desires but to serve Him with renewed hearts and purpose. As Jesus promised His disciples power, that same power is accessible to us today. It's the power to serve God, to move in His direction, and to fulfil the Divine purpose for which He created us.

Pray This With Me

Dear Jesus, envelop me in the love of Christ and empower me, Holy Spirit, to walk in Your ways. Deliver me from all that hinders my connection with You. Open my eyes and ears to comprehend You deeply. Lord, help me to truly know Jesus better, to live and exemplify His teachings. Let our lives reflect the love You have bestowed upon us. Transform our character to radiate love instead of hatred, embodying the purpose You've destined for us. Amen. Thank You, Father, for Your love and grace. We honor and glorify Your name, Jesus. Amen.

Printed in Great Britain
by Amazon

38778506R00088